BE AN ACHIEVER

A Handbook to Get Things Done

GEOFFREY MOSS

KOGAN PAGE

Acknowledgements

My thanks to all my friends and colleagues, in many countries, who have shared their experiences and ideas with me in this book. Special thanks to my wife Joyce for editing my script.

Copyright © Moss Associates Limited 1990

First published in New Zealand in 1990 by
Moss Associates Limited, 7 Dorset Way, Wadestown,
Wellington 1, New Zealand.

This edition first published in Great Britain in
1991 by Kogan Page Ltd, 120 Pentonville Road,
London N1 9JN.

British Library Cataloguing in Publication Data

A CIP record for this book is available from the British Library.

ISBN 0-7494-0582-1

Typeset by DP Photosetting, Aylesbury, Bucks
Printed and bound in Great Britain by
Biddles Limited, Guildford

Contents

Acknowledgements 4

Preface 9

1. Advice From Achievers 11

2. Get Started 15
Write your own obituary 16
Where would you like to go? 16
What do you want to achieve? 16
What is your secret ambition? 18

3. Plans, Principles and Priorities 21
Plan your future 21
Plan your work 23

4. Smart Ways to Get Things Done 31
When do you work best? 31
Don't become a perfectionist 32
Make fast decisions 32
Capture your fleeting ideas 32
Keep records 33
Win the paper war 33
Use the six D system 34
Answering letters 34

5. Time-wasters and Trivia   **35**
Procrastination 35
Overcoming procrastination 35
Interruptions 36
Overcoming interruptions 36
Time-wasters 37
Dealing with time-wasters 38

6. Helpful Checklists and Hints   **39**
Agenda for a formal meeting 39
Audience analysis 40
Borrowing money for a business 41
Brain-storming 45
Career choice 46
Chairing a meeting 48
Conference or convention planning 49
CV 51
Delegation 52
Dictation is easy 53
Displays and exhibitions 54
Fax and telex messages 55
Impasse 57
Interviews when applying for a job 57
Interviews when selecting staff 58
Introducing a speaker 60
Job satisfaction 61
Leadership 61
Lectures 63
Letters to the editor 68
Listening 68
Media support 70
Meetings 72
Negotiation 72
Problem-solving 73
Questions 74
Reports 75
Stress 80
Supervision 81

Telephoning tips *82*
Thanking a speaker *84*
Time-saving tips *85*
Training *86*
Travel *91*
Visual aids *95*
Write for easy reading *96*

Preface

One day I was interviewing a top executive of a large corporation. When we got chatting he told me:

> 'Early in my career I missed out on a senior promotion. I really wanted that job. I knew I was the better candidate and I could do a better job. I was determined to prove the selection panel wrong.
>
> Looking back, that was a turning point in my career. Adversity often makes you determined to succeed. I worked hard and step by step I climbed the corporate ladder. The person they selected now works for me – I'm his boss.'

We can make things happen if we are prepared to work hard, study, plan, accept criticism and move around to gain experience and confidence.

Set-backs can be turned into positive forces and make us more determined to succeed.

I believe in the power of positive thinking. Great things are possible if you have confidence in yourself. If you believe you can do something, you are well on the way to success.

Life is like going up steps. Each new experience is an additional step. But make sure you are going up all the time and not slipping backwards.

Be an Achiever

Each person is unique and ambitions are unique to each person. This book was written to help you achieve your ambitions.

It will show you how to get things done. It will help you to get a reputation as a doer. Chapters 3, 4 and 5 contain simple and practical recommendations which can be easily adopted. Chapter 6 gives specific checklists, basic principles and helpful hints for many tasks an achiever must carry out.

If you have a dream, this book could help you to achieve it.

CHAPTER 1
Advice From Achievers

I once asked an influential businessman what he thought was the secret of his success.

'If I have learnt one thing over the years, it's no one owes you a living. If you want something you must be prepared to work hard and give something in return.'

Since then I have asked many successful people what advice they would give to those wanting to succeed in their careers, hobbies or personal life.

The head of a large government department gave this advice:

'At any early stage I learnt one basic fact. Never seek credit for yourself. If you want to bring about change and get on in this world, let someone else get the credit for your ideas – in the end you will benefit. Feed your ideas to your boss. Let him or her pass on your ideas to the politicians and get the votes. Ultimately you will be rewarded.'

Here are other recommendations:

'First impressions are important. Pay attention to grooming – the way you dress, the way you speak. Dress for the job you want, not the job you are in now.'

'Always have an aim. Keep a diary and write down what you

hope to achieve. If it is a big goal break it down into short-term goals and set time limits. We work best when we challenge ourselves with a deadline.'

'Work hard at what you can do best. No matter how humble your job, aim to be the best in your field. You'll become the expert in that field.'

'If you are competent, people will have confidence in you.'

'To succeed you must believe in yourself. Confidence and enthusiasm are contagious and are the main reasons why most people succeed.'

'Become a doer not a talker – get a reputation for getting jobs done. Meet deadlines and get a name for reliability. Listening is important, too – always make an extra effort to hear your boss out.'

'Be curious. Learn to ask simple questions. Don't take anything for granted.'

'Search for basic principles and common truths. Try to pare things down to the bone. Don't be afraid to ask, "What is the real purpose of this organisation I work for? Is it to make money for shareholders, give a public service, or what?". . .'

'Most people lack confidence in themselves. It's getting experience to build up that confidence that's important. That's where travel and taking responsibilities in social clubs can help. We set our own boundaries and limits largely by confidence in ourselves. If you believe you can do a job, or you believe you can do a job, or you believe you can't, you are probably right.'

'Always look forward. Look to the future – don't worry about past failures. Situations change. You can't live in the past – it's the future where you are going to spend the rest of your life.'

'Be optimistic. Always look for the positive side of things. Don't be narrow-minded – be forward thinking. If you have a few knock-backs, don't get depressed. Bounce back with increased vigour.'

'Seek successful people to advise you – cultivate them and ask how they became successful. Most successful people like to share their experiences – it appeals to their ego!'

'If you want to be a successful manager there's one thing you should remember. That's the golden rule and it's still the best advice I can give you: Always do unto others what you would like them to do unto you.'

CHAPTER 2
Get Started

After you have read this section you should be able to decide on your goals and then plan your work and study to achieve them.

People can be put into three categories:

- those who make things happen
- those who watch things happen
- and those who wondered what happened.

What category are you?

Achieving is like travel. Before you start on a journey you must know your destination. Before you can achieve you must know where you want to go. You must plan your route and predict your difficulties and challenges. Break your journey into easily achievable stages. The sooner you start the sooner you arrive at your goal. Don't be afraid of going slowly. Be afraid of standing still.

'If you don't know where you are going, you can't get there.'

Getting started is half the battle.

Sit down quietly by yourself, or go for a long walk and think about your achievements.

Write your own obituary

Pretend you are writing your own obituary. What have you accomplished so far in your life – what successes are you proud of?

Now list . . .

1. Your talents and skills
2. What you like doing best
3. Jobs you enjoy most.

Is it possible to cash in on your talents and interests or develop your skills further?

Where would you like to go?

Next, make lists of what you are doing now and where you would like to be in five years' and in ten years' time.

What do you want to achieve?

- To excel in a sport?
- To run a marathon?
- To be an accomplished artist, potter, musician, public speaker?
- A satisfying, challenging, interesting, highly paid job?
- A happy marriage with a family?
- To travel widely?
- To be the head of your department or the managing director?
- To own your own home?
- To own a boat?
- To manage and own your own business?
- To make a million pounds?

and so on. Ambitions are unique to each person.

Write these down in your diary or planning book where you can refer to them.

CAREER
Today:
Five Years:
Ten Years:
FINANCES
Today:
Five Years:
Ten Years:
QUALIFICATIONS AND WORK EXPERIENCE
Today:
Five Years:
Ten Years:
PERSONAL LIFE
Today:
Five Years:
Ten Years:

This simple exercise will help you to start your plan.

What is your secret ambition?

Whatever you decide, write it down on a card. Carry it in your handbag or wallet. Look at it frequently and think of ways to achieve your goal. Visualise yourself as a success. As soon as you believe your goal is attainable, you are ready to start planning. You must believe in yourself and be determined to succeed.

To excel in any sport requires hours of practice so you must be prepared to sacrifice a great deal of social life. Successes against the clock and against competitors will give you confidence to strive for even better performances.

To become a great musician, artist or public speaker needs hours of regular study and practice. You must always strive to do better. Welcome helpful criticism and always evaluate each effort. The rules are simple – it's the sacrifice and dedication that are hard.

It may take time to get the sort of job you want. Be prepared to move from job to job until you find the one you want. Job satisfaction is a worthwhile goal. You may even have to change countries. But be fussy and don't sell yourself short.

A happy marriage means a wise choice to start with and constant effort. Remember it is a sharing situation and you must be prepared to give if you want something in return.

You will need money if you want to travel widely. If you want to work in a foreign land, you will need skills. People with nursing, teaching and computer skills usually have little trouble finding work in other countries.

To be a manager you need to develop not only management skills but also leadership skills. You should also act and dress for the part. You must be reliable and be able to get things done in line with the policies and objectives of the organisation you work for.

You can often develop leadership skills through working on

committees of social or sporting clubs. The more work you put into a committee the more experience you gain. Serving on school boards or training in military reserve units can help to develop your skills. Go and work for an organisation that has a progressive training and leadership development policy. Many international companies have excellent training programmes.

To own your own home, boat, car or business you will need money and a good credit rating. This is usually best done by becoming established with one banking organisation but don't hesitate to shop around for the best competitive deal.

To own your own business you may need to learn new budgeting and accounting skills. Personal contacts are also important.

Before you buy any business you would be wise to work for a good boss, in a similar business, in the district you have chosen.

If you plan to buy a car dealership, work on one in the district to get local knowledge and local goodwill.

When starting, keep your overheads low. Ask yourself, 'How can I get the biggest return from the money I am spending?' You don't need new equipment to start a business. Look for good used machinery to keep your costs low.

If your ambition is to make a million pounds or more, you will need capital to get started. The best way to start is to save. Invest a percentage of your earnings each pay day.

You will need to develop investment and accounting skills. Employ a good accountant and lawyer (the best you can find) but remember they are only your advisers. You will make the final decisions and take the risks. If you are determined and prepared to learn from your mistakes (and other people's) anything is possible.

Review your plans from time to time. Conditions change and as you gain confidence and experience, your plans will need to change too.

'Thinking always ahead, thinking always of trying to do more, brings a state of mind in which nothing seems impossible.'

Henry Ford

CHAPTER 3
Plans, Principles and Priorities

After you have read this chapter you will be able to plan your work to achieve your goals.

When you have decided what you want to achieve, you must start planning how to go about it.

The time you spend planning is a sound investment because it will save you much time later.

Plan your future

Your plans, like your ambitions, will be unique, but there are certain principles that will help you.

- Take a long-term view. Your ambition might involve years of study.
- Aim for job satisfaction.
- Plan each step of your career carefully.
- You will have to be prepared to manage your time well and allow time to study, to earn more money, to learn more skills and so on.

Your choices – if you need more time for these activities
1. Work longer hours
2. Work more efficiently
3. Do only important work.

1. Work longer hours

You could set aside an hour or two at the beginning or the end of each day for study or extra work. This way you may get through more work but you may get tired and the quality of your work could suffer.

2. Work more efficiently

You can do more work in the time available with strong discipline. You must become something of an efficiency expert – watching time, motion and deadlines. But make sure your staff relations don't suffer. Commitments and deadlines do get work done but don't overdo them.

3. Do only important work

With this approach, list your activities and set out your priorities. Perhaps you can break your tasks into 'essential', 'necessary' and 'non-essential' jobs.

WORK PRIORITIES JOBS		
Essential	**Necessary**	**Non-essential**

Forget about the non-essential jobs; do the important tasks.

Give essential jobs priority and set deadlines for their completion. Get rid of those pleasant but non-essential jobs. If you value your time, delegate time-consuming, detailed work. Highly paid seniors are paid to think and lead, not to do mundane tasks – even if you do enjoy the work.

Concentrate on your more important tasks – your high priority ones.

Look for objectives and basic principles
To become an achiever look for basic goals, objectives and principles. Keep things simple. Don't put too much emphasis on procedures.

People are often judged by how well they comply with procedures and directives. This causes reports to multiply and clog up an organisation. Instead, we should judge staff by how well they meet goals and objectives.

Look for basic principles. They are beliefs or guidelines that are universal truths that apply anywhere and at all times.

'A public service department is a department set up to service the public.' This is a basic principle that is often forgotten.

If you are in business to make a profit watch your overheads.

Plan your work

What is your job?
Before you look at techniques to reduce work pressure and get things done you must know precisely what your job is.

What are you paid to do? What responsibilities have you? Have you a job specification? When was your job specification last reviewed? Have things changed since then?

Many people are vague about their work responsibilities and are afraid to ask. If you are not sure, ask your supervisor for an up-to-date job specification.

If you are self-employed, go away and do some thinking. Try some old-fashioned meditation. What 'game' are you really in. What are you trying to do? Get down to the basics. List all your jobs and try putting them into priority order. Question routine procedures to see if they are still relevant and necessary.

Determine your work load
Make time to take stock of all the jobs you do.

Try listing everything you do each day for a week – including interruptions.

List telephone calls, casual visitors, meetings and suchlike. At the end of the week analyse your jobs by listing and categorising them into essential, non-essential and time-wasters.

Ideally you should do only essential work. Trivia and time-wasters can clog up your working day.

Budget your time
There is one thing we all have in common – we all have a 24-hour day. It's how we use that time that's important!

What do you do when you can't cope with the volume of work?

- You must set your priorities for your jobs. Make choices and assign one activity ahead of another.
- Get rid of unnecessary tasks.
- Budget your time carefully.

If you are in a managerial position, you should always make time to talk and listen to clients and staff – this is the most important part of some jobs. If staff have a problem, stop what you are doing and listen to them. Budget for this time.

If you are to become an achiever, develop the skills of listening to others and asking simple open-ended questions.

Make sure you also budget time for family and recreation.

All work and no play makes Jack or Jill a dull person.

> **Today work smarter – not harder!**

Budget your resources
With new ventures think of the costs. Think of the alternatives. Think of the benefits in money and other terms. Location is important. Where do you want to work? Where do you want to live? Then draw up your plan listing the resources you will need.

Set your priorities
Focus your energy on what you hope to achieve.

We all have different priorities and different responsibilities. My priorities go first to my family, then to my employer and everything else rates third.

A German colleague told me this story to illustrate responsibilities.

A friend came home recently and his wife told him confidentially that the woman in the flat above was having an affair.

'Well that's *her* problem,' he said.
'But, I was told it's with you!'
'Well that's *my* problem.'
'If that's all you have to say I'm going home to live with Mother.'
'Well that's *your* problem!'

Your responsibilities will determine your priorities.

There are two ways of setting priorities: according to urgency or according to importance.

Most people set them according to urgency and never start a project until they reach a deadline. They spend most of their time 'putting out fires'.

Set your priorities in order of importance.

An action plan

Take your high-priority, essential jobs and plan what action should be taken, the time required and the dates when they should be completed.

Here is a suggested plan:

Objective	Task	Method	Time required	Target date
What do you want to achieve?	What is to be done?	How will it be done?	How many hours? days? weeks?	Date when job must be completed

Good working habits
Get a reputation for getting things done.

Don't become a butterfly, flitting from one job to another.

Do each job well and finish it before going on to the next.

Concentration and self-discipline improve with practice.

One job at a time
Don't get side tracked.

If you can sort out your priorities and do only one job at a time you make better progress.

If you are working on a difficult task and someone interrupts you, don't stop and do their job. Try being more assertive and say, 'Please come back after lunch when I have finished the job I am working on. I will help you then.'

Most of us tend to take the easy way out. We make excuses and postpone difficult and time-consuming tasks. The longer we put off a big job the harder it becomes. We make excuses – we are too busy, or the job is too big to start just now.

Tackle jobs step by step
Here is a simple technique that can help you to become an achiever – and it works every time.

> **Carve big tasks into small bites and deal with only one bite at a time.**

Specify what you want to do, set yourself a time limit and try to keep to it. Don't be too ambitious at the start – be realistic.

By completing one step of a difficult task you encourage yourself to tackle the next step. It doesn't matter what the job is, whether it is preparing a report, writing a book, developing a business or painting a house. Try it – it works!

Many self-made people started in a small way. They set high standards and made a success of one small business, learning from their mistakes and the mistakes of others. They finished up with a chain of shops, motels, hotels, restaurants or other services. Some have even been able to franchise their business.

Decide on basic units
Good units are an hour, a day or a week.

'For the next hour I will . . .'
'Today I will complete . . .'
'Next week I will do the following jobs . . .'

Start by taking one day at a time. Then each day becomes a step towards your goal or goals.

Make time to think and get organised.

Some 'early birds' like to plan first thing in the morning; others prefer the end of the day. Keep your plan simple and flexible. As Murphy said, 'Anything that can go wrong, will go wrong', so be prepared to adjust your timetable.

Your priorities will also change from time to time. Don't worry as long as you are heading in the right direction.

Recommendations
- Clear your office desk before you go home each night.
- Today make a list of jobs for tomorrow.
- Decide on the order you want to tackle them.
- Try to complete your tasks one at a time.
- Transfer any jobs not done to the next day.
- Start the day by doing the most unpleasant things on your list. You will feel relieved and exhilarated. The sense of achievement will encourage you and set the tone for the rest of the day.

Plan each day

Here is a simple, cheap idea that could make a big difference to your reputation as an achiever.

Get a small notebook. (5 × 8 cm is a convenient size to fit in a shirt pocket or a handbag.) Used pages can be torn out easily if it has a spiral binding.

On the front cover print:

TODAY'S JOBS (in priority order)

and on the back cover print:

JOBS TO BE DONE (with realistic deadline dates)

Make this notebook your 'Daily Planner'. Keep it with you all the time.

Use a fresh page each day. Transfer your long-term plans from the back to the front when the day arrives for action. Add any of the previous day's jobs that didn't get done.

A notebook is more reliable and easier to work than an electronic diary. It is not a substitute for your desk diary – it is a memory jogger and planner.

Some people prefer cards to a notebook. Small filing cards are easy to carry and can also fit into a small holder on your desk as a visual reminder of the day's jobs.

Make every day a day of achievement.

CHAPTER 4
Smart Ways to Get Things Done

A colleague in Sri Lanka noted for his hard work and the long hours he spent on the job would often say:

'No bees, no honey.
No work, no money.'

People who work hard are usually successful. But there are many smart ways to reduce effort and still become an achiever.

When do you work best?

Identify your peak working hours and use them wisely.

Some people are 'early birds'. They get up early and are most creative during the tranquil morning hours. The first few hours at work are peak times for some. If you are one of those don't waste this time doing routine jobs such as reading a newspaper or the mail, or making routine phone calls. Others work best late in the afternoons or in the quiet of the evening. They have been called the 'owls', and the early starters, the 'fowls'. Are you an owl or a fowl?

Allow time to 'warm up' to creative work. Reading a stimulating book or article helps. Many people drink coffee or tea, others go jogging or walking or exercise in other ways.

Try scheduling your high-priority work for the times you work best. Avoid too many interruptions during this period – protect your peak time.

Don't become a perfectionist

Never spend more time on a job than it warrants. Being a perfectionist often means becoming a procrastinator. You want a reputation for high standards but don't waste valuable time.

Make fast decisions

Get into the habit of making decisions quickly. As soon as you have all the necessary facts, act! Indecision only causes worry to staff and clients.

The head of a large government department put it this way:

'Decision-making is like learning tables in arithmetic. With practice, you develop the ability to make quick decisions. And once you make a decision, forget it. Don't worry whether you have made the right decision; don't come back to it – just go on to the next job.

'Set yourself deadlines. If you are committed to deadlines and tell other people about them, you are more likely to stop procrastinating and get jobs done.'

Indecision is usually the worse mistake you can make.

Capture your fleeting ideas

Good ideas come and go – catch them while you can. We get good ideas at the most unexpected times. If you capture them you can build up a bank of ideas to reconsider later.

Remember the little notebook, your daily planner. Carry your notebook always. Keep it beside your bed at night. It will always be handy to jot down any thoughts or inspirations.

Some people use a tape recorder to capture their ideas while driving their car; others carry a planning diary. The important thing is to catch and record your fleeting ideas before they slip away.

Keep records

Develop a good filing system and keep a diary. By keeping accurate records of your meetings, travels, business transactions and financial deals you will reduce your work stress. They can save you time, worry and money when you write reports or claim expenses.

> **A place for everything and everything in its place.**

Win the paper war

You need a simple, effective filing system, a good retrieval system and a big waste-paper basket.

Incoming post should be sifted and sorted quickly. Try standing up to do this job – you will do it faster.

An assistant or a secretary can save you time by sorting your post. Do the job with them periodically, so they know your requirements.

Don't file useless or 'dead' information.

Throw out all unwanted ('junk') mail. Every piece of paper you retain in the filing system creates further work and confusion. Don't end up with unwieldy trivia-loaded files!

Try to avoid a 'pending further action tray' for low priority jobs. You may intend to do them when you have some spare time. You never will!

When in doubt, throw it out!

A paperless computerised system with a back-up has some advantages but there are certain things which will always have to be put on paper.

Use the six D system

1. Drop junk mail into your waste paper basket.
2. Decide what action has to be taken on each letter the first time you read it.
3. Delegate to the appropriate person to answer.
4. Delay action by filing letters (with appropriate 'bring up' dates) into folders.
5. Determine priorities. Which letters will you answer first?
6. Deal with letters methodically.

Answering letters

As you read a letter use a highlighter to pick out the key questions to be answered. Make notes in the margin to help you dictate replies.

If possible, action a letter the first time you pick it up.

Your secretary should be able to answer routine letters and collect references for you.

A file of 'model' letters on a computer disk can save much time, but try to personalise each letter.

CHAPTER 5
Time-wasters and Trivia

Your main enemies are procrastination, lack of planning, interruptions and lack of concentration. They stop you getting things done.

Procrastination

- Don't put off unpleasant tasks.
- Make an effort to do jobs when they should be done.
- Develop good working habits and time-saving systems.
- If you feel you should do a job, get on with it – otherwise you will start to worry about it.
- The world is cluttered up with unfinished projects that have been put aside to be done later.

Overcoming procrastination

- If you have clear goals and objectives and you know what you should be doing, it's easy to get started.
- Break jobs into small workable tasks. Try the 'divide and conquer' method.
- Prepare a plan. List the steps you will take.
- Set deadlines. Budget your time.
- Commit yourself. Tell others your plan.
- Get started – now!

> **'Tomorrow is often the busiest day of the week.'**
> Spanish proverb

Interruptions

You can deal with unscheduled interruptions in two ways. You can either try to get rid of them or budget time for them.

Your choice will depend on the importance you place on the need to listen to clients and to staff or your desire to get work done.

A friend was especially busy trying to meet a deadline for an important report. The voice from the corridor was that of a talkative acquaintance. To avoid interruptions and in utter desperation my friend crawled under his desk.

The receptionist ushered the visitor into the room.

'That's strange!' said the receptionist. 'He can't be far away. He was here a few minutes ago. Would you like to wait?'

With that they sat down and began to talk – and talked, and talked – for nearly an hour.

My numbed friend eventually emerged from his cramped quarters, very stiff and very embarrassed.

He told the story against himself and vowed it would never happen again. He would face up to his time-wasting problems and learn how to deal with interruptions.

Overcoming interruptions

Try to eliminate interruptions or delay them so they don't interfere with your peak-time priority work.

- Improve your office communications to reduce questioning from staff. Use circular letters, newsletters, video messages, conference phone calls and meetings.
- Schedule meetings so staff can ask questions and discuss policy matters.

- At meetings, start on time, get to the point quickly and keep to the agenda.
- Train your secretary to 'filter' visitors and phone calls.
- Plan for a quiet period free from interruptions each day.
- Escape to a 'secret' quiet room to do planning and creative work.

'There are three things that can never be retrieved – the spoken word, time past and the neglected opportunity.'

Old Muslim saying

Time-wasters

Look for these time-wasters:

- Unscheduled meetings
- Unnecessary meetings
- Too many reports
- Too many rules
- No priorities
- No clear objectives
- Out-of-date job specifications
- No time plans
- No deadlines
- Attempting too many jobs at once
- Interruptions (telephone calls and unscheduled visitors)
- Poor filing system
- Low staff morale
- Lack of procedures for routine jobs
- Failure to delegate
- Filling in non-essential questionnaires
- People with pet projects
- Unclear requests
- Lack of feedback
- Lack of information
- Procrastination

- Too much reading
- Junk mail

and so on.

Dealing with time-wasters

1. Mark your time-wasters.
2. Which ones waste the most of your time? Place them in priority order.
3. Take your number one time-waster and see what you can do to overcome it. Then move on to your next-time-waster.

By tackling one problem at a time you will progress. Try it! See also *Time-saving tips*, page 85.

CHAPTER 6
Helpful Checklists and Hints

To be an achiever, you must know clearly what you want to do and how you are going to do it.

Here are some useful checklists and hints to help you get things done. If a new task is thrust upon you or you have to organise an event, use them to check the basic principles and read the practical tips. They will make your life easier and save you time.

Key words have been chosen for the initial words in the titles and the lists have been arranged in alphabetical order of those words.

Agenda for a formal meeting

Keep to a sequence:

1. Open the meeting
2. Apologies
3. Welcome new members and guests
4. Minutes of previous meeting
5. Business arising from the minutes
6. Correspondence
7. Business arising from correspondence
8. Financial report
9. General business of which notice has been given
10. Reports from committees
11. Business arising from reports
12. Other general business – with consent of the meeting

13. Notices of motions for future meetings
14. Announce date and time of next meeting
15. Close the meeting.

(See also *Meetings* and *Chairing a Meeting*, pages 72 and 48.)

Audience analysis

Do your research. Before you start preparing to address a meeting or give a presentation, find out as much as possible about your audience.

Composition
- How many will be present?
- What is the age range?
- Will you be speaking to all women, all men or a mixed audience?
- What are their occupations?
- What is their economic position?
- What is their social status?
- What educational levels have they achieved?
- What are their racial backgrounds?
- Are there any language limitations?
- Is the audience derived from a club, an organisation or a specific group?

Beliefs, attitudes and values
- Will they have strong prejudices?
- What are their religious beliefs?
- What are their political views?
- What are their values?
- What are the accepted norms in their social behaviour?
- Will they have special interests?
- What will motivate them?

The occasion
- What is the occasion? Why were you asked?
- What are the aims and objectives of the organisation?

- What does the audience already know about your subject?
- What will be their attitudes towards your views?
- What will be their attitudes towards your background and position?
- What will they want to hear?
- What messages do you want to give them?

Appeal to the audience's beliefs, attitudes and values.

Borrowing money for a business

Start with a plan. Many new businesses fail because they are under-capitalised. It is easier to borrow money at the start of your new business venture than when things begin to go wrong.

Planning your case

- Your success will largely depend on a well thought out business plan and on your reputation.
- The more comprehensive your plan the better your chances of getting a loan.
- Prepare a background statement about your business, setting out objectives, ownership, assets, staffing, location, markets and services.
- Persuade lenders their money will be safe. Show that it will be used to earn a good profit and you will be able to repay capital and interest on time.
- Budget for contingencies.
- Produce evidence of the demand for your products and services. Market survey figures will help your case.
- Include copies of your accounts for the last three years.
- For new ventures prepare a feasibility study giving a cash flow analysis showing your predicted income and profit and loss figures.
- Get reports to support your case from your accountant and other appropriate professionals.

Lenders will look for:

1. Your assets so they can get their money back if things go wrong
2. A commitment from you
3. A realistic budget allowing for all possible contingencies
4. Your ability to repay loans.

Information you should give the lender:

1. The reasons for borrowing the money
2. The amount you need
3. Your marketing plans
4. Your pricing formula
5. Your starting budget
6. Your cash flow forecast for the next three years
7. Your audited balance sheets for the last three years.

Preparing your business plan

A plan will help you to clarify your ideas and assess the project more objectively. Once you have your ideas on paper it will help you to raise money and permit you to monitor the project once you start.

- If you are using your plan to raise money the document should be crisp, neat and free from errors, with an attractive cover.
- It should contain all relevant names and addresses including those of your accountant, solicitor and bank.
- It should be well set out, easy to ready and written in the third person.
- Make a clear statement outlining the project and its objectives. Include the reasons for borrowing the money.
- Give the business history of the firm and the management. Include the date of incorporation (if a limited company) and the qualifications and experience of management and staff.
- Give the company's financial position with audited figures for the last three years and the budgeted plans for the next three years.
- Describe the product or services your business will be offering. Include photos if appropriate.

- Summarise your market research. Give the size of the market. What competition is there? What advantages do you have over your competitors? The more accurate the figures the better.
- How do you intend to advertise, promote and sell your product and services?
- Name your distributors, suppliers and subcontractors.
- State the type of premises you have or require, with geographical location.
- List the equipment you have or need, and the age of your machinery.
- Describe the vehicles you have or need for transport.
- Do you need planning permission or a licence to get started?

Predicting and monitoring results

There are three types of financial statements essential in business.

1. Profit and loss accounts
2. Cash flow forecasts
3. Balance sheets.

Your accountant will be able to help and advise you during their preparation.

1. Profit and loss account

This summarises your income and expenses over a set time and should include the following items:

- Income from sales or services
- Cost of goods or services sold (include the stock you had at the start less the stock at the end).
- Gross profit or gross margin. (This is the difference between your sale profits and the cost of the goods or services.)
- Operating expenses (include all your costs).
- Profit before income taxes
- Income taxes
- Net profit (your actual profit or loss after paying tax).

2. Cash flow forecast

This is a summary of the money you expect to receive and pay out during a set time. Here is an example:

CASH FLOW FORECAST from .... to ....

CASH IN	JANUARY		FEBRUARY etc	
	Forecast	Actual	**Forecast**	Actual
SALES				
LOANS				
OWNER'S CAPITAL				
OTHER MONEY				
TOTAL CASH IN				
CASH OUT				
STOCK				
WAGES				
RENTS				
TAXES				
RATES				
INSURANCE				
ELECTRICITY				
TELEPHONE/TELEX/FAX				
TRANSPORT				
PRINTING				
ADVERTISING				
STATIONERY & POSTAGE				
ACCOUNTANT				
OVERDRAFT INTEREST				
LOAN REPAYMENTS				
PETTY CASH				
SUNDRIES and so on				
TOTAL CASH OUT				
NET CASH FLOW				
OPENING BALANCE				
CLOSING BALANCE				

3. *Balance sheet*

This is a summary of assets, liabilities and your equity in the business at a specific date. It shows what the business is worth.

> You can have a great plan and work very hard but if you can't get backing, if you can't get money when you need it, you can't get anywhere.

Brain-storming: Generating ideas to solve problems

If a group is faced with a difficult and complex problem, you can use a brain-storming session to help solve it.

1. Choose a leader who is enthusiastic and able to stimulate the group.
2. Start with some warm-up exercises, eg ask the group to list all the uses for a common object such as a brick. You could run a competition to see who could suggest the most uses for a bucket if you were marooned on a desert island.
3. Make sure the group understands what is meant by brain-storming. Ask them to 'free-wheel' to get as many ideas as possible, no matter how crazy they may seem. Tell them there must be no comment or criticism of ideas at this stage.
4. Select one or two members to write up all the ideas on a board so the whole group can see them as ideas flow.
5. Define the problem in simple terms. Probe for the real causes.
6. Set deadlines.
7. Ask for ideas – as many as possible. The greater the number, the greater the chance of coming up with a solution. Don't allow interruptions or negative comments. Take a break as soon as enthusiasm declines.
8. After the break examine each idea to see if it has a practical application. Try putting solutions into priority order.
9. Discuss and compare them. Look for ways to combine or improve ideas.

10. Decide on the best solution.
11. Plan how it can be put into practice and discuss implications.

'Imagination is more important than knowledge.'
Einstein

Career choice

Job satisfaction is important.

Plan your career
If you are entering the work force, you need:

- A good basic education. Don't specialise in subjects at school too early – leave your options open.
- A variety of work experience. Work in different holiday jobs; take part in work experience programmes.
- A variety of social experience. Join clubs, participate in sports and, if possible, travel, so you meet many types of people from different social and ethnic backgrounds.
- Career counselling and guidance.
- A plan of what you want to do and how to go about it.

What are you good at?
First identify your interests and strengths. Make four lists.

1. Your academic qualifications and your special talents
2. Jobs you enjoy most
3. Things you do best
4. Jobs you dislike doing most.

Start looking for a career that would make the best use of your qualifications, experiences and talents and has the most tasks you enjoy and the least tasks you dislike.

What sort of life style do you want?
Think about the standard of living you would like and decide

what you will have to do to achieve it. You may have to compromise between what you enjoy doing and your financial needs and ambitions.

Take a long-term approach
Be prepared to take a long-term approach to a career. This might involve years of study at a university or polytechnic. Join organisations that have strong training programmes and good career paths and ones which allow employees paid time off to study. Ambitious people often have better prospects if they join large businesses or international organisations.

Get professional advice
Get advice from career counsellors – they have been trained to help you. You don't have to take their advice but they can give you leads, confirm your ideas or suggest alternatives.

Get work experience
Before you settle on a career get as much work experience as possible in a variety of jobs. Take holiday jobs in different areas and in different countries if possible. Try working in a hotel, a shop, an office or a factory, until you find a job you enjoy. That will give you a lead towards your career.

Overcome your weaknesses
First identify your weaknesses. If you want to set up a business and you lack the necessary skills, make an effort to learn from someone who has these skills. Go back to college, to a technical college or a university or polytechnic. Be prepared to study, regardless of your age. Read books, attend seminars, join clubs to help strengthen areas you will need in your future career. For example, if you want to be a teacher you will need strong leadership and communication skills as well as technical skills. If you make up your mind and you are determined enough, you will succeed.

Get your foot in the door
Make the most of any contacts you have to get started in the

organisation you would like to work for. If you have none, dress smartly, take your personal fact sheet and talk to the personnel manager. Ask to be put on their waiting list for future jobs. Keep in contact with the personnel manager. Don't wait for them to call you. Telephone often or call in to see if any positions are becoming vacant. Be willing to take a temporary job, a holiday job or a mundane job to get started. Work hard and show people you are ambitious and keen to work your way up in the organisation.

Don't get in a rut
If you are not happy in your job, change it. There are plenty of jobs if you have the talent, qualifications, skills and the determination.

Make big plans. Small plans arouse little enthusiasm.

Chairing a meeting

Before the meeting, the chairperson should:

- Be familiar with the constitution or bylaws.
- Know the minimum number (quorum) that must be present to conduct business.
- Know the correct voting procedures and whether notices of motions need to be given prior to the meeting (and if so, how many days before).
- Prepare the meeting agenda with the secretary.
- Make sure the secretary has given due notice of the meeting to all members.
- Read the minutes of the previous meeting to see what business needs following up.

At the meeting
- Start (and finish) on time.
- See whether a quorum is present.

- Call the meeting to order – formally.
- Keep to the agenda.
- Keep speakers within the rules of the meeting procedures.
- Preserve order and courtesy.
- Remain neutral during debates.
- Keep a sense of humour. Keep calm. Do not dominate.
- Call speakers in the correct sequence after they have indicated they wish to speak.
- Decide on points of order.
- Prevent irrelevant and repetitious discussions.
- You may appoint committees and exercise a casting vote.
- You should not refuse motions if they have a seconder. But you may rule for or against the following motions:

  'That the question not now be put.'
  'That the matter be referred to a committee.'
  'That the debate be adjourned.'
  'That the meeting now adjourn.'
  'That the Chair's ruling be dissented from.'
  'That the meeting no longer has confidence in the Chair.'

- Summarise and reach conclusions so things get done.
- After the meeting, follow up and co-ordinate to see that things get done.

> **A chairperson must have the ability to make different opponents appear as if they belong to the one team.**

Conference or convention planning and organisation

Before you start
Before you start organising a conference or convention, answer these questions:

1. Why is the conference being held?

2. What are the aims of the organisation and the objectives of the meeting?
3. Who do you hope will attend?
4. How many people will you be able to accommodate?

Your working committee

- If you are the organiser your job is to co-ordinate activities. Don't try to do all the work – delegate jobs to others.
- Select your working committee carefully. Pick people who have the time and the ability to get things done.
- Call a meeting of these people and if they agree to take on a responsibility, give them instructions in writing.

'Mr Alan. You are responsible for all publicity. Your job is to . . . You have the authority to set up your own working party and to delegate jobs to others. You are responsible for seeing things get done and reporting progress at the meetings of the organising committee.'

Tasks to consider

- What is your theme?
- Choose speakers.
  Know what topics you want discussed.
  Know how speakers will perform on these topics.
  Will they be compatible with your audience?
  Will they draw an audience?
- Contact speakers.
  Phone first to see if they are available and to answer their initial questions.
  Follow up with a letter confirming dates, times, subject, transport and accommodation arrangements.
- Prepare programme.
- Book meeting rooms.
- Book accommodation for speakers and guests.
- Arrange publicity.
- Arrange catering.
- Organise signs, decorations.
- Arrange for a sound system.

- Organise visual aids, projectors, screens and emergency equipment.
- Check on availability of seats and tables.
- Organise registration staff and facilities.
- After the event:
  Write to thank speakers.
  Pay accounts.
  Evaluate conference and make a note of changes for next time.
  Write reports.
  Get follow-up publicity by supplying the media with stories.

> **The success of a conference can be measured by the level of discussion and the action that follows.**

CV (Curriculum Vitae): Your personal fact sheet

The first thing you should do when applying for a job is to prepare your personal fact sheet, called your CV or resumé.

It should be typed neatly and well set out on good quality A4 bond paper. Employ an experienced typist if necessary.

Keep it simple and as short as possible. Attach a recent photograph – one where you are smartly dressed.

Attach photocopies of appropriate certificates and references.

Your CV should contain the following information:

- Full name and address
- Telephone number – day and evening
- Nationality
- Age, date and place of birth
- Marital status
- Educational qualifications

- Work experience
  Dates, names and addresses of employers, type of work, your
  responsibilities and accomplishments
  Holiday jobs
  Voluntary community work
  Give details of skills relevant to the job you are applying for, eg
  computer, accountancy or foreign language skills
- Hobbies, sports and interests
- Leadership experience in sport, youth groups, community
  projects, etc.

Give names, addresses and phone numbers of three people who
can supply references. (Be sure to contact these people first to get
their permission.)

Those who do not hope to win have already lost.

Delegation

A manager can delegate jobs:

- To have more time for important jobs
- To train staff
- To test staff in different situations.

If you delegate to reduce your work load, match the staff to the
jobs you want them to do.

For successful delegation:
1. Make sure the task is achievable.
2. Explain why the job is important.
3. Give clear instructions. If they are complex write them out in
   plain English.
4. Give the staff authority to act.
5. Tell staff what results you want.
6. Agree on a deadline.

7. Make sure they know who to go to for help, if they need it.
8. Don't interfere while they are doing the job.
9. Ask for feedback and regular progress reports.
10. Be helpful and positive when you receive the reports. Counsel the staff if necessary.
11. Praise good work.

It is easier to satisfy your superiors than those under you.

Dictation is easy

When work pressure builds up, you can save time by dictating letters and reports. Getting started is hard. Here are some tips to help:

- Make sure you have all the relevant papers before you start.
- Make brief notes for the replies you intend to dictate. See that your notes are in logical order.
- Try to put yourself in the position of the person receiving the letters.
- Avoid interruptions as much as possible – cut off the telephone, for example.
- Treat your secretary with consideration. Explain the nature of the work, the type of document you require, how urgent it is and whether you require a draft. Encourage your secretary to ask questions.
- Start by dictating short letters. Use full notes until you gain confidence.
- Go over each sentence mentally, before you dictate it. It must sound right to the ear. Pretend you are actually speaking to the person you are writing to. Avoid slang and jargon.
- Speak clearly, exaggerating the pronunciation of words. Spell proper names and technical terms. Be considerate – don't dictate too quickly. Try to keep up a constant speed with an occasional rest. Don't mumble with your hand in front of your mouth. Don't talk with anything in your mouth.

- Try not to interject with asides when you dictate.
- Don't walk around the room when you dictate.
- Indicate the end of each paragraph.
- If you have papers for your secretary place them in the same order that you dictate.
- Say who is to sign the correspondence and give their designation.
- Specify the people who are to receive extra copies.
- Ask for a rough draft only if you plan to alter or revise letters.
- Don't be hesitant about asking your secretary for advice. Secretaries can be a big help when you are learning new office skills.

'Next to doing a good job yourself the greatest joy is in having someone else do a first-class job under your direction.'

William Feather

Displays and exhibitions: Rules for success

Displays and exhibits must get their messages across quickly. They should arouse interest, stimulate thought and cause action.

Guidelines for a successful display:

1. Specify your aim. What do you want your viewers to do?
2. Catch your audience's attention with a gimmick.
3. Try to get people involved – competitions are good.
4. Tell them your message. Keep it simple and crystal clear – in basic English. The fewer words the better.
5. Give a handout to those who are interested. (Simple useful gifts are good memory-joggers.)
6. Make follow-up calls to people who show interest and want further information.

If you don't stop them . . . you don't sell them.

Fax and telex messages save time and money

Business messages sent by facsimile (fax) and telex machines have certain advantages over telephone messages. They are usually cheaper, they imply urgency and they provide permanent copy. The same message can be sent to many addresses and the fax machine can also send illustrations, diagrams and photographs.

Fax and telex machines use different networks so many organisations have both for back-up services.

If you send short messages within a country, telex can be cheaper than fax, but fax is faster and cheaper for international messages.

Telex messages are accepted by law and are usually preferred by banks, hotels and conference centres for confirmation of deals and bookings. Telex messages are typed in capital letters so are slower to read. They are more reliable for business transactions in countries where telephone reception is poor.

Tips for using a fax machine
- If you are using a machine for the first time, read the instructions.
- Make sure you know the way to insert the document. (This varies with machines.)
- Preset your machine for no more than two 'redials'. If you are not getting through, the lines could be overloaded, so wait and try later.
- Define your subject precisely with a bold heading.
- Make the message as short and as clear as possible.
- If any documents are torn, repair them and photocopy before you send them.
- If your copy is faint, photocopy to darken it, or set your machine to low contrast.
- Use 'halftones' for better reproduction of photos and drawings.
- Check the fax number, name and full address of the recipient.

(Wrong numbers are costly if you are calling internationally.) Commonly used numbers should be stored in 'auto dial' to reduce the possibility of mistakes.

- Check your name, address, telephone number, telex and fax numbers.
- Read your draft for clarity and omissions. Check for logic. (If it is an important message, test it on a colleague to see if it is clear.)
- Repeat important figures in words.
- Put the date at the beginning of your message.
- Indicate the number of pages you are sending.
- Type or print your message. Hand-written messages are often hard to read.
- Advise contacts if you change your fax number.

To save money
- Use simple letterheads with outlines. Don't use bold, blocked logos.
- Don't use thick lines.
- Keep your messages as short as possible.
- Use abbreviations, eg plse for please, attn for attention, tks for thanks.
- Don't put your address or a commercial at the bottom of your paper. If you have a short message you will be charged for the white space between your message and your address.
- If you have information on only half the page, cut the page and send only half.
- If you are disconnected during your message, stop, put the document back in the machine and call the operator and explain what happened. You will be reconnected and your account should be adjusted immediately. (It is difficult to argue a month later when the account comes in.)
- You can reduce international charges by using a 'delayed send' to make use of cheap rates.
- Don't make your fax number too widely known. You could be inundated with junk mail and thermal paper is expensive.

- Keep your activity slips in a logical order. Use them to check your account.

Get attention at the beginning of your message.

Impasse: Dealing with a deadlock

When further negotiations seem impossible:

- Adjourn to rethink and consult.
- Review progress, stressing the positive side of negotiations.
- Restate common concerns.
- Write up issues and developments for all parties to study and think about.
- Consider the outcome if negotiations don't continue.
- Say honestly how you feel about the situation.
- Ask, 'What if we do this . . . or that?' Be prepared to give something if you want something.
- Talk about positive past relationships and how both parties have benefited.
- State the long-term benefits of an agreement and what the consequences will be if agreement is not reached. State negative results concisely and clearly.
- Move to a different issue to give time to think about the consequences of an impasse.

If everything fails
- Set a date for another meeting and walk out.

You only fail when you give up.

Interviews when applying for a job

Do your homework thoroughly. Find out about the organisation you are hoping to join. Annual reports are a good starting point. Talk to staff. Make an appointment and find out what they do – staff trainers and employment officers can be helpful. Ask for a copy of the job description and work out your responses if asked how you would cope with the jobs on the list.

- Dress suitably – the way they would want you to be dressed if you were working for them. Don't wear dark glasses – interviewers like to see your eyes.
- Be punctual. Arrive early so you can relax and be composed for the interview. Often a walk before the interview helps you to relax.
- Take references, CV and certificates in case they are needed, but don't flaunt them.
- Be polite. Wait until you are asked to sit. Sit up straight – no smoking or chewing gum. Smile, and be natural – don't put on an act.
- If you are asked, be prepared to say why you would like the job and what you hope to contribute. Be modest and honest.
- Show you are enthusiastic and keen to get the job.
- If you do not understand a question, say so. If you cannot answer a question, say how you would find the answer. If you cannot do a task, say you are willing to learn.
- Don't take over the interview. Let the interviewers ask the questions. Try to answer concisely and be prepared to amplify if asked. Don't talk too much.
- Your job is to sell yourself. Be friendly, be natural, be enthusiastic, be ambitious about your work and outside interests. Show you are an interesting person.

First impressions are important.

Interviews when selecting staff

Successful staff selection starts well before an interview. Write a job description. What work do you expect the person to do? List tasks, working conditions, responsibilities, relationships, designation, etc.

- Next, write personal qualities needed for the job – appearance, health, knowledge and skills, intelligence, expectations and values, etc.
- List the topics you want to cover. Where appropriate, devise short tests of relevant skills.
- Select a pleasant quiet room for the interview. Minimise disturbances; put a 'meeting in progress' sign on the door and stop all telephone calls.
- Before the interview, while the candidates are waiting, arrange for someone to look after them. Make them feel welcome – give them a cup of coffee, talk to them and show them around.
- When they enter the interview room, introduce them and make them feel at ease. Make small talk and let them relax before you move into the serious interview. Your object is to help them to talk freely.
- Ask questions in everyday language. Get the candidate talking by asking open-ended questions or inviting comments. 'Tell us what you have done since you left school.'
- Encourage the candidate to ask questions about the job or organisation, but don't lose control of the interview. Working conditions should be clearly explained and understood.
- Never let a candidate leave an interview feeling demoralised even if he or she is unsuitable. Candidates should be told they lack the skills required in a way that maintains their self-respect.
- Make notes after each interview.
- Decide on an appointment as soon as possible. If you need to check any details, use the telephone – it's surprising what people will tell you over the phone.
- Contact the successful applicant with a job offer. Find out when he or she can start work. Once the successful candidate has accepted, thank the unsuccessful applicants as soon as possible and keep a list of their names and addresses in case you need them later when other vacancies arise.

Recruit staff with skills needed to strengthen your organisation. Aim to build a team with different skills. Do not recruit clones.

Introducing a speaker: Create interest

If you are asked to introduce a guest speaker tell the audience briefly what the subject is and why the speaker has been chosen to talk about it. You should 'sell' the speaker to the audience. Get your audience interested in the speaker and the topic. Create an atmosphere that will make the speaker want to perform well and the audience keen to listen.

Introduce the audience
As well as introducing the speaker to the audience you should introduce the audience to the speaker. 'In this club we have many business leaders and they are keen to hear your ideas on new marketing ventures.'

Give qualifications and experience
Tell the audience about the speaker's qualifications, position and title. Don't give a complete biography, just the parts pertinent to the speech or things that reinforce the authenticity of the subject.

Give the speaker's name as the final part of your introduction.

Make the speaker feel welcome
Lead the applause, keep looking at the speaker and continue clapping until the speaker is ready to begin.

Remember
- Be brief. Be lively. Be sincere.
- Don't be over-enthusiastic or too flattering.
- Avoid clichés such as, 'Today's speaker needs no introduction.'
- Don't talk about yourself or your opinions.
- Never apologise if your speaker is a substitute for the one you wanted.

Be brief, sincere, enthusiastic and seated.

Job satisfaction

Enjoyment in your work results when you achieve things:

- When you are given interesting, challenging and creative tasks.
- When you are given responsibility.
- When you have a good boss who appreciates you.
- When you are rewarded and praised for good work.
- When you feel part of a team.
- When you really believe in a cause and you know you are doing a good job and making a worthwhile contribution.

Satisfaction comes from a job well done.

Leadership can be learnt

Leaders are not born, they develop. They are able to influence, guide and shape the attitudes, expectations and behaviour of others. Leadership is largely a behavioural skill, so you can learn it and develop it yourself. You can become a better leader by studying, practising and asking for constructive feedback from your colleagues.

Here are some suggestions to help you develop as a leader:

- Make the most of every opportunity that comes your way. Accept responsibility at work and in professional and social organisations. Volunteer for tasks. Be prepared to work hard for long periods when called upon.
- Develop an enthusiastic loyalty to your employer and organisations you support. Take a pride in belonging and offer constructive suggestions for improvements.
- Be prepared to work with little or no supervision. Make decisions and use your initiative.
- Set high standards. Leaders can be recognised because their staff produce superior work and have a higher output.

- Be ambitious. Stretch yourself by setting goals and objectives and work to achieve them.
- Learn the skills of people management. Take time to listen to people's complaints, ideas and suggestions. Try counselling and helping staff with personal as well as work-related problems. Delegate work and praise good work - give credit when credit is due.
- Develop team leadership skills by improving your communication and training skills. Attend seminars and training classes and read widely.
- Develop your social skills. Make an effort to mix easily with different types and races of people. Study different cultures and religions. Learn to ask open-ended questions and to develop your listening skills. Dress suitably for occasions. Copy peer dress habits - you will feel more comfortable and are more likely to be accepted.
- Keep calm in times of stress. Avoid producing stress in others and try seeking their help to remove causes of stress. Good communication should help to remove causes of stress.
- Make an effort to be flexible. Try adjusting your behaviour to meet the experience, knowledge and skills of others in every situation.
- Inspire people to achieve. Expect results.
- Focus attention on the important issues.
- Delegate, giving clear directions and guidelines. Trust staff and don't interfere.
- Accept people as they are. Approach problems and relationships as they are at present, not as they were in the past.
- A good leader does unto others what you would like them to do unto you.

'In the simplest terms, a leader is one who knows where he (or she) wants to go, and gets up, and goes.'

John Erskine

Lectures

Here are three checklists for:
1. Preparing a lecture
2. Delivering a lecture
3. Getting more from a lecture.

Preparing a lecture
Check these things before you write your lecture.

Audience
- Who are they?
- How many are expected?
- What are their worries, concerns and interests?

(See also *Audience Analysis*, page 40.)

Expectations
- How much time will you have to speak?
- Will there be questions?
- Do you need to prepare a handout?
- Will reporters be present?

Environment
- Where will you be speaking?
- When?
- Are there other speakers? (If so what are they talking about?)
- What other business is on the agenda?
- Is there a lectern if you need one?
- Will you need a microphone?
- Are there facilities for visual aids?

Topic
Your topic is . . .

Purpose
Your purpose is to . . .

   introduce
   thank
   support
   inform
   instruct
   convince
   inspire
   motivate
   get action
   entertain.

Aim (Objective)
Your aim is . . .

What responses do you really want?

Lecture outline
What is your main message? (Write it down very briefly.)

Then organise your most important points and supporting statements.

- Your first main point leading to . . .
- Second point, leading to . . .
- Third point etc.

Conclusion
- Summarise your main points.
- Give a memorable message.
- Call for action, if appropriate. (Appeals must be realistic.)

Now go back and write your introduction.

Introduction
- Get attention.
- Arouse interest.
- Reveal purpose of talk.
- Establish a rapport with your audience.

Next decide on a title.

Title
- Make it interesting, intriguing and appealing.

Add an explicit subtitle if necessary.

Visual aids
What visual aids do you need to reinforce the message?

They must be simple, understood and seen by all!

Some of the most effective are:
Overhead projector
Slide projector
Video
Movie projector
Demonstrations
Boards (white, chalk, flannel, chart)
Handouts
Models
The real thing.
(See also *Visual aids*, page 95.)

Warnings
1. Spoken language is different from written language. Rewrite articles or reports in suitable language.
2. Lectures should never be read. After you have written out the spoken version, pick out key memory words and speak to them.

A speech is like a journey – it has purpose, direction and an ultimate goal.

Delivering a lecture
- Dress for your audience. Your clothes should be comfortable and suit the occasion.
- Before you are due to speak get the 'feel' of the room and the

audience. Sit at the back of the room and observe other speakers and the reactions of the audience.

- During a break, check the sound system to get your levels right and to see how you adjust the microphone height.
- When you get up to speak take time to compose yourself. Adjust the lectern, arrange your notes, adjust the microphone, take a deep breath, look the audience over, smile at a friend and when you are ready, start.
- Always address the Chair. The preferred forms of address are 'Mr Chairman' or 'Madam Chair'.
- The way you begin is very important. That's when you establish your credentials and build a rapport with your audience.
- Don't read; talk to your audience. Use key words as memory joggers.
- Share your feelings. Talk about your experiences and emotions. Be enthusiastic about your subject.
- Watch your audience. Can they all hear you? If they look bored tell them a story. If they look weary give them a break.
- If you 'dry up' don't panic. Ask for questions or pause and compose yourself – make it look like a natural break. Then start off on another point.
- Use good visual aids – they can save you a lot of explaining. But they must be simple and seen by all.
- Your conclusion is very important. It is the last chance you will have to leave a memorable message. Spend time preparing your conclusions fully.

The end should be a climax, not an anti-climax.

Getting more from a lecture
Here are some ways to learn more from a lecture.

Before the lecture
Read as much as you can about the topic.

Select your seat carefully
Choose a comfortable seat, away from distractions. Make sure you will be able to hear the speaker clearly and see all the visual aids.

Give your undivided attention to the speaker
Concentrate on what the speaker is saying. Watch for body language. Listen for areas of interest. Listen for new information. Ask yourself, 'What's in this for me?'

Make brief notes using your own form of shorthand
Jot down headings to increase your recall.

Look for 'facts' and 'principles'. Don't write down details or you will miss cues.

Keep an open mind
Don't stop listening because of your preconceived ideas or your biases. 'Emotional blackouts' make you lose the thread of the talk.

Don't create distractions
Don't talk to people sitting near you or try to make clever remarks. Don't read or doodle – look at the speaker.

Keep asking yourself questions
Use the five Ws and two Hs – who, what, why, when, where, how and how much.

Keep summarising and reviewing
Weigh up the evidence as it is presented.

Ask the speaker questions
Ask the speaker if you do not understand something or if you want further information.

> **'He who asks a question is a fool for five minutes – he who does not, remains a fool for ever.'**

Letters to the editor

Free publicity for your ideas can be obtained by writing letters to the editors of prestigious newspapers.

Here are some guidelines:

- State your ideas or complaint clearly at the beginning of your letter.
- Don't be offensive. You will get more impact with restrained language than with abuse.
- Use humour and satire. They often hit where it hurts most.
- Avoid topics such as religion and racial controversy, blasphemy and issues which could be libellous.
- Start with an attention-grabbing introduction and your strongest argument. Arrange your statements in logical order. Leave your weaker arguments to the end because that is the part that will be left out if the letter is too long, or space is not available.
- Keep your sentences and paragraphs short.
- When you have drafted your letter, 'boil it down'. Remove all jargon, clichés and all unnecessary words.

> **'A good rule for letter writing is to leave unmentioned what the recipient already knows – tell them something new.'**
> Sigmund Freud

Listening

Improve your listening:

Stop talking
You cannot listen if you are talking – and if you are talking you are not learning.

Put the speaker at ease
Encourage the speaker. Try putting the speaker's feelings into

words. 'I am sorry to hear my decision has upset you. I do appreciate what you are telling me. Tell me what we can do about the problem.'

Show that you want to listen
Look and act as if you are interested. Give full attention. Show you are listening. Nod and make encouraging remarks. 'Yes, I see what you mean.'

Remove distractions
Shut the door, turn off the radio, don't doodle or walk about.

Empathise with the speaker
Try to put yourself in the speaker's shoes and see his or her point of view. 'Why did he say that? What would I have said?'

Be patient
Allow plenty of time for listening when you make appointments. Don't interrupt. Don't keep looking at your watch.

Control your emotions
If you get emotional you will not hear properly. You will get the wrong meanings from words and you could get the wrong message.

Go easy on argument and criticism
Ask questions to draw the speaker out. 'Why did you say that? Is that what you really feel? What facts have you to support that statement?' Don't argue or attack. If you put speakers on the defensive they may 'clam up' or get emotional.

Ask questions
Questions encourage the speaker and show you were listening. Ask questions for amplification. It helps to develop a topic. Ask: 'Why do you believe that?'

Summarise, review and reflect
From time to time summarise what you think the speaker has

said and repeat the speaker's words. This will help the speaker and help you remember.

Media support

Work for mutual benefits. To be an achiever, sooner or later you will need the support of the media to get your ideas and messages across to your target audience. To do this you must understand the role of the media and the needs of reporters. Both the print and the broadcast media are in the business of making money and meeting deadlines.

The reporter's job is to gather and report news. Try to understand the difficulties of the job and the struggle to meet deadlines set by the editor. Today's news is history tomorrow.

If you want publicity for your cause or your business you will need to take the initiative. It is your job to make contact with reporters if you have a message to get across. Make sure your message is news, not propaganda or free advertising.

Helping reporters
- Give as much advance notice as possible of forthcoming events. Follow up with reminder calls.
- Supply copy if possible. Make your messages as clear and concise as possible and enclose background material.
- Type your message on one side of the paper only.
- Double space the typing leaving wide margins.
- Leave a large space at the top of the first page.
- Put your name and telephone number on the top of the first page.
- Number the pages clearly.
- Never break a paragraph going from one page to the next.

Be cooperative
- If a reporter wants a story, try to help – you may need help one day.
- Try to give accurate, factual information.

- If you do not have the information, suggest where it might be found, or offer to get it. If you say you will call back at a certain time, keep your word. Remember, journalists have strict deadlines to meet.

Foster good relations

- Make a special effort to establish good working relationships with reporters. Be honest with them and work to build up mutual trust. Good media relations take time and effort but they pay dividends.
- Give reporters leads for stories. Prepare your material well for them. Give them good briefings and supply accurate information.
- Misreporting often occurs because people do not take time to explain what they really mean – they take things for granted.
- If you are misquoted, contact the reporter first and try to discuss the problem in a friendly manner. If you storm into the editor's office you will lose the reporter's respect and cooperation.

Coverage of events

- Send advance detailed information to the editor as soon as possible.
- Keep following up with newsworthy, human interest stories as they develop. The names and achievements of distinguished guests can make interesting reading and publicise your event.
- On the day of the event, make life easy for reporters. Arrange for them to have a table and a light near the speaker. Supply them with a programme and copy of the speakers' papers. Arrange for someone to act as their host and give them any help they require. Often they need a quiet room for typing up copy.

Hints from experienced journalists

- Hard facts stop speculation. You can kill criticism and stop rumours with a timely, honest, factual story.
- Never say 'No comment' unless you want a full investigation carried out.

- When you come out of a meeting, be prepared to answer tricky questions. Being unprepared is a sure way to get a bad press.
- Don't be upset if a reporter uses a tape recorder – it helps to get your story right.

> 'A controversy with the press in the press is the controversy of a fly with a spider.'
>
> Sir Henry Taylor

Meetings

Run better meetings:

- Call a meeting only when it is necessary.
- Plan and prepare yourself for all meetings.
- Have clear and achievable objectives.
- Prepare and distribute an agenda early.
- Keep to starting and finishing times.
- Keep control. Know the rules, give clear directions, listen carefully, summarise often and keep on schedule.
- Get things done. Action by whom? By when?
- Make the most of the talent and experience present.
- Review and summarise often.
- Record recommendations and give members responsibilities for specific tasks.
- Evaluate meetings. Can we do better next time?

(See also *Agenda for a formal meeting* and *Chairing a meeting*, pages 39 and 48.)

Negotiation

Negotiating is conferring with another party with the aim of reaching an agreement.

1. Try to look at things from the other side's point of view.

2. Look for options where there are mutual gains.
3. Look for problems below the surface – not the obvious problems, the unspoken ones.
4. Try to separate people and personalities from the situation.
5. Always consider the economics of the various solutions.
6. Focus on mutual interests, not on non-negotiable positions.
7. To gain something be prepared to give something.

Hints
- Do your homework thoroughly and plan a strategy.
- Write down what you want to achieve and your bottom line. Then try to do the same for the other side.
- Be polite and ethical and *never* lose your temper under any circumstances.
- Emphasise common concerns and points of agreement.
- Seek information by questioning to probe and clarify issues. Use basic language where possible.
- Respect confidentiality of talks and asides, and express appreciation for the other side's time and efforts.
- Weigh up and evaluate options. 'These are the consequences if we do this or that.'
- Keep discussions on track and moving. Write up issues and interests for all to see and think about.
- Make a special effort to listen carefully, especially for hidden meanings. Jot down reminder notes.

'If you are patient in one moment of anger, you will escape a hundred days of sorrow.'

Chinese proverb

Problem-solving

Find out what the real problem is. It is not necessarily the obvious problem. There may be historic or personal considerations. Look for alternatives.

- Don't rush from defining the problem into solving it.

- List all possible causes.
- Brain-storm for possible solutions. (See also *Brain-storming*, page 45.)
- Use lateral thinking.
- Discuss and examine every idea for immediate or future use.
- Choose the best solution.
- Plan the action required to implement it.
- What will be the implications?

Concentrate and the world is yours.

Questions: How to get more information

Most successful people have mastered the art of asking questions. It is a skill worth developing.

- Use questions to help the other person think and develop ideas.
- Ask open-ended questions to encourage people and to help put them at ease. These questions also draw out more information from people.

'Why did you take up teaching as a career?'
'What made you go to North America?'

Closed questions rarely get more than one or two words in reply.

'Where were you born?'
'How long have you worked here?'

- Start with 'comfortable' questions to establish rapport. Ask about mutual acquaintances, hobbies, sport or other interests.
- Use key words to get facts – what, why, when, where, who, how and how much.
- Ask 'suppose' questions.

'Suppose you were the boss. What things would you change?'

- Try 'probe' questions.

    'You said you were not happy about the job. Why is that?'

- Ask 'agreement' questions.

    'How would it be if we tried such and such?'

- Ask for evidence, examples or explanations to discover reasons behind a person's thinking.

    'Why did you say that?'
    'Give me an example?'

- To encourage others to think or to avoid committing yourself to an answer, return the question.

    'That's an interesting question. Why did you ask me that?'

To be an achiever, try using these simple questioning methods.

Reports

Report writing can be an interesting and exhilarating experience. It's your chance to help bring abut change. It is not a difficult job if first you break it down into small tasks.

The master plan
- Ask for clear terms of reference:

    Who are you doing it for – who will read it?
    What are the objectives?
    What size report is expected?
    When is it due?

How much help can you expect from other people?
What size budget have you?

- Where can you collect the background information?
- Who do you need to interview? What are you going to ask them? (Prepare your questions.)
- How are you going to record and sort new information – using a card system, sheets of paper or computer disks?
- Set out a realistic timetable for each step of your plan.

Preparing your report
Your first task is to collect all the available information from files, libraries, interviews and retrieval systems. Sift the relevant from the irrelevant – be ruthless but keep a record of references.

Organising your material
- When you have collected all the material you require, arrange it in a logical order.
- Don't confuse facts and opinions. If it is a fact, say so; if it is an opinion, assess its value.
- Appropriate information goes into the body of the report; relevant supporting material goes into the annex or appendix.

A basic structure
Time is valuable to top management so keep your report brief, to the point, factual and easy to read.

Here is a basic structure for a well set out and comprehensive report.

1. Title
2. Table of contents
3. Abstract (or summary)
4. Introduction
5. Main body
6. Conclusions
7. Recommendations
8. Acknowledgements

9. References
10. Appendices (or annexes).

Title
- Make the title factual, clear and brief.
- Include key words – for computer reference systems.
- Preferably use less than 12 words – you can always add a subtitle.
- The title page should include details of the author, the name and address of the organisation and the date.

Table of contents
List all the major headings and subheadings, appendices and illustrations with page references.

Abstract (or summary)
Write this last. It is really a mini-report giving the basic facts, the evidence and the conclusions. It should be a single paragraph of approximately 200 words.

Introduction
State the purpose of the report. The introduction usually includes the terms of reference and defines the reasons the report was written.

Main body
It should be easy to read. It should give a comprehensive and systematic review of the subject, the evidence and the possibilities. There should be a logical sequence leading from topic to topic.

Careful paragraphing, subheadings and numbering will help make it easier to read.

Attractive layout creates a good impression and encourages reading.

A suggested layout:

1.0 MAJOR HEADING

1.1 Sub-heading

1.1.1 First point
1.1.2 Second point
1.1.3 etc.

1.2 Sub-heading

2.0 MAJOR HEADING

2.1 Sub-heading

2.1.1 First point
2.1.2 Second point

and so on . . .

Conclusions

- Busy people may read only the conclusions and recommendations; therefore they should be simple, concise and complete.
- The conclusions should be clear statements derived logically from the main body of the report and supported by relevant evidence.
- They should be arranged in order of importance and should relate to the purpose of the report.

Recommendations

Recommendations for future action should be stated simply and concisely. Make sure they are positive, practical and cost effective. They should be numbered in order of importance or logic. (They are sometimes put at the beginning of a report.)

Acknowledgements

Thank people or institutions for their help in the preparation of your report. (Acknowledgements are sometimes put before the table of contents.)

References
For books, list:

> Author (or authors): Surname and initials or given name
> Year of publication
> Title of book
> Edition, if applicable
> Publisher
> Place of publication
> International Standard Book Number (ISBN)
> Page number or numbers, if applicable.
> > eg Moss, Geoffrey, 1991, Be an achiever
> > Kogan Page Limited
> > London ISBN 0–7494–0582–1

For journals, list:

> Author (or authors): Name first, then initials and title
> Year of publication
> Title of article
> Title of journal or periodical
> Volume number and part or issue number
> Page number or numbers.

Appendices (Annexes)
This section should contain supporting material such as sets of data, details of methods used, graphs and illustrations.

The material should be chosen and presented with the same care and logic as the rest of the report – it is not a dumping ground to fill out a report.

Attractive presentation
- Ask a colleague to edit your report – spelling mistakes, lack of logic and verbosity can spoil a report.

- An attractive cover and good layout make a favourable first impression.

Follow up
Don't take it for granted the key people will read your report. Take the initiative and make an appointment with them to discuss your findings and to answer questions.

> 'Find out everything everybody else knows, and then begin where they left off.'
> Thomas Edison

Stress: Reduce it

When your body tells you are under stress, take stock of your lifestyle. Try to think through the causes of your stress. They may be pressure of work, a difficult boss, marital problems, financial worries, peer pressures or many other things.

For serious problems you may need urgent counselling and professional advice – there are many people who can help you.

If you are under stress you could try some of the following:

Go for a relaxing holiday
Forget about work but think about your future.

Reorganise your lifestyle
- You may need to change your environment – your job, your town or city.
- You may need to get away from your peers if their social pressures are too great.
- You may need to change your accommodation if it is unsatisfactory.

Make time to relax
- Take control of your life and budget your time for periods of

relaxation. Use this time for reading, listening to music, meditating, or just to plan your next day. Some people relax by drawing or painting, gardening or doing craft work.

- Learn relaxation methods to ease tense muscles.

Exercise regularly
- Take up a sport you enjoy such as golf, tennis, fishing, boating or swimming.
- You may prefer jogging or running, or working out in a gymnasium.
- Go for long walks.
- If you are not an active sportsperson, follow a sport you enjoy watching.

Make an effort to have fun
- Do more of the things you enjoy doing most. Join clubs or take up activities that interest you.
- Try to plan your work better and budget times for fun.
- Don't take life too seriously – try to turn tense situations into games or challenges.

Keep healthy
- Make sure you have a sensible, healthy diet with plenty of whole grain foods, fresh fruit and vegetables.
- Aim for moderation in all things. Restrict your intake of caffeine (in coffee and tea), be aware of the dangers of smoking, and don't abuse alcohol or drugs. (Tranquillisers should be taken only under medical advice.)
- There are some excellent stress management programmes so don't hesitate to get professional advice if you need help.

Supervision

1. Employees must always understand clearly what is expected of them.
2. They must have guidance in doing their work and know who they can go to for advice.
3. Good work should always be praised or rewarded in public.

4. Poor work should be criticised constructively, out of the hearing of other people.
5. People should have opportunities to show they can accept greater responsibilities.
6. People should be encouraged to improve themselves.
7. People should work in a safe and healthy environment.

How to be a good boss
Tell your employees:

- What is expected of them.
- Who they are responsible to.
- How they are performing.
- How they can improve.

Telephoning tips

Make better use of your telephone.

To save time
Keep a list of frequently called numbers by your telephone. Many telephones have built-in memories for numbers and automatic re-dial buttons.

- You can take notes when you talk if you use a hands-free telephone or a shoulder-fitting device which clamps to your telephone handset.
- A telephone answering tape recorder can record messages for you. With some machines you can receive your messages when you are travelling by dialling your home telephone number and using a code number.

Business calls should be planned
Before you place a call, list the points you want to cover or questions you want to ask.

Impressions depend entirely on what is heard
Smile before you talk and try to found friendly and enthusiastic.

Perceptive listening is important
Listen for voice tone and inflections, to tell if your contact sounds busy or preoccupied. If so, offer to call back.

Don't do all the talking
Pause from time to time. Give the other person time to think and respond.

Call your contact by name
If in doubt, ask the telephone operator the name of the person you will be talking to.

Make your calls at convenient times
Get to know people's work habits. For international calls, allow for differences in time zones and daylight saving times.

When calling long distance
Tell the operator who answers where you are calling from. This encourages prompt action.

- Keep frequently used references handy to the telephone. If an incoming call requires further research, don't keep the caller waiting. Offer to locate the information and phone back at a specific time.

If clients call with complaints
Be sympathetic – do not cover up with excuses. Thank them for bringing the problem to your notice and offer to investigate and call back. Investigate as soon as possible, phone back and explain what you are going to do about the problem.

When selling over the telephone
1. Identify yourself and your organisation.
2. Establish rapport.
3. State and dramatise the purpose of your call.
4. Arrange a personal visit or demonstration.
5. Conclude on a friendly note.

Involve your switchboard operator

Switchboard operators are usually the first contacts people have with your organisation. They are very important people. Train them well. Keep them informed of staff responsibilities, dates, times and places of meetings, names of publications and activities of the office or department. The more you involve them the easier they will make your job.

Keep the operator informed of your movements

If you cannot be found when an important long-distance call comes through, you could lose business.

> **The telephone is one of the most effective time savers and one of the biggest time wasters.**

Thanking a speaker

Speak for the audience.

When a guest speaker has addressed a meeting, the audience usually show their appreciation by passing a formal vote of thanks.

Be prepared

If the chairperson has asked you earlier to move a vote of thanks to the speaker, you can be prepared and if necessary make notes during the speech. At the end of the speech the Chair will probably give you a nod and you then stand. Speak up so all can hear you.

'Mr Chairman, I have much pleasure in moving a vote of thanks to Mrs Ross for her interesting talk tonight.'

Show a lively appreciation of what was said. Comment on a few points of interest in the speech and the manner of presentation. Show you enjoyed the speech – try to speak for the audience. Be brief, be witty. Thank the speaker sincerely and modestly. Do not criticise the subject matter even if you disagree with it. Finish with:

'I wish to move a vote of thanks to Mrs Ross.'

Vote of thanks
The Chair puts the motion to the audience and it is usually carried by acclamation (clapping).

See also *Conference or convention planning* (page 49) and *Chairing a meeting* (page 48).

Time-saving tips

Get things done in the office.

- Are you sure you know what your job really is – your responsibilities and your duties?
- Check on your work load – list inessential jobs and time-wasting procedures.
- Become conscious of time, without undue anxiety.
- Constantly plan your work.
- Strive for goals and objectives.
- Look for techniques that best suit your style of work.
- Cut red tape to the minimum.
- Identify your peak working hours and use them well.
- Commit yourself to responsible tasks.
- Try to get your priorities right – important jobs first.
- Practise making fast decisions.
- Don't become a perfectionist.
- Sift and sort incoming post fast, into priority order.
- Action a letter the first time you pick it up.
- Keep model letters for routine replies.
- Learn to dictate.
- Computerise lists for commonly used addresses.
- Index commonly used fax, telex and telephone numbers.
- Don't file useless information.

- Develop a reliable filing and bring-up system.
- Try to complete one job at a time.
- Don't put jobs off – complete them as soon as you have the facts.
- Keep your desk clear of clutter.
- To overcome procrastination, break big jobs into segments, set deadlines, tell people about them and start work.
- Cultivate systematic habits.
- List working procedures, rules and policies to be followed.
- Learn to read fast and efficiently.
- Identify information-rich sources and use abstracting and review services.

Training

- Train and develop staff. Take every opportunity to ensure that staff regularly learn new skills.
- As a career step, consider becoming a trainer.
- Training programmes need careful planning and preparation if they are to be successful.
- Check the following steps in your training programme.

1. Analyse the job.
2. Analyse the trainees.
3. Assess the training needs.
4. Set training objectives.
5. Select and organise the content of your programme.
6. Select training techniques, methods, aids.
7. Prepare lesson plans.
8. Decide how the programme is to be evaluated.
9. Carry out training.
10. Evaluate.
11. Review programme and revise if necessary.

Planning is the key to success

1. Job analysis
Describe the job. What qualifications does the worker need to do the job?

- What does the worker do?
- Why?
- How?
- How well?

2. Trainee analysis
Who are they? What can they do already?

- Who/Where are they?
- Special characteristics
- Level of knowledge/skills/experience?

3. Training needs assessment
What are their weaknesses? How can you help them to overcome these weaknesses?

- List weaknesses and ways of overcoming them.

4. Determine training objectives
These describe what trainees should be able to do at the end of their training that they could not do previously.
What changes do you want? When do you want it? How much change? How will you know?

- What has to be done?
- Under what conditions?
- Up to what standards?
- How will it be evaluated?

Remember your ABCD:

A Audience – Who are you going to train? Be specific.

B Behaviour – What type of change do you expect?

C Condition – When and under what conditions do you expect this change to occur?

D Degree – How much change do you expect and how will you find out?

An objective must:

- Describe the final results.
- Be specific and precise.
- Describe a change that is measurable or observed.
- List criteria against which success can be measured.
- Mention essential conditions under which results can be achieved.
- Specify an end point.

5. *Select and organise content*
Decide on the content of the training programme. Organise content in logical order.

- Study source of information.
- Decide on content.
- Organise content in logical order.

6. *Select training techniques, methods, aids*
Decide which training techniques, methods and aids you will use.

- Decide on appropriate techniques.
- Select suitable methods.
- Decide on training aids required.

7. *Prepare lesson plans*
Allocate the use of your time and plan step-by-step activities.

- Decide how each lesson is to be presented.
- Set out each lesson step by step.
- Allocate time for each activity.

8. *Plan evaluation*
A good evaluation will help you to do better next time.

- Decide on information required.
- Decide when this should be collected.
- Study methods of gathering information.

- Select method to be used.
- Prepare questions which have to be answered.

9. Conduct training
Encourage participation and use a variety of training methods.

- Keep to your lesson plans.
- Use a variety of methods.
- Encourage participation.
- Use demonstrations, models, visual aids.

10. Evaluate training
Make sure you get honest feedback.

- Conduct planned evaluation.
- Summarise results.
- Write evaluation report.

11. Review and revise
Strive to do better next time.

- Summarise training.
- Review in the light of evaluation.
- Discuss with other trainers involved.
- Revise to improve relevance.

Training ways – use imagination and a variety of methods
Here are some commonly used training methods:

Audience reaction team
Brain-storming
'Buzz' session
Case study
Committee
Conference
Convention
Debate
Demonstration

Discussion group
Drama spots – role playing
Exercise
Exhibit
Field trip
Film
Forum
Interview
Lecture
Listening team
Multi-media package
Panel
Peer teaching
Programmed instruction
Question time
Seminar
Short course
Skit
Symposium
Teleconference
Tour
Video-television
Visit
Workshop

Which training ways should you use?
Variety is important! To transfer knowledge, use:

- Group discussions (questions and answers)
- Group or individual exercises
- Lectures (with handouts)
- Forums
- Panel discussions
- Films, videos etc.

To solve problems, use:

- Case studies

- Brain-storming
- Discussion groups
- Exercises etc.

To develop skills, use:

- Demonstrations for manual skills
- Role playing for interpersonal skills
- Peer teaching
- Programmed instruction etc.

To change attitudes, use:

- Debates
- Displays
- Role playing (for clarifying how others feel)
- Group discussions (for group attitudes)
- Individual exercises
- Demonstrations
- Campaigns etc.

The aim of training should be to inspire action rather than fill with knowledge.

Travel

Tips for trips:

- Research and plan your trip by talking to people who have travelled in the countries you plan to visit.
- Deal with an experienced, well established travel agent.
- Make sure your passport is valid. Obtain any necessary visas and check that vaccinations are up to date. Carry spare passport photos for any visa applications you may need later.
- Before you leave, check if the countries you are visiting ban visitors who have travelled to certain countries. (Some

countries ban people who have visited Israel or South Africa.)
You can overcome this problem by asking for visas on loose
pages or by getting a second passport.

- Find out about the seasonal climate at your destination. This is
especially important if you are visiting areas with a monsoon
climate. Spring is often a good time to visit in temperate
regions.

- Write a detailed checklist of essentials to pack – clothes, toilet
gear, medication, camera. Here is my checklist:

Suits (mix and match)
Comfortable clothes for lounging
Shirts
Ties
Underclothes
Socks (cotton for hot climates)
Comfortable shoes, sandals and shoe cleaning gear
Nightwear
Swimwear
Rainwear
Handkerchiefs and/or tissues
Toilet requisites
Small medical kit
Torch
Travel alarm clock
Small radio (to pick up BBC World Service in foreign
countries)
Diary, maps, stationery
Plastic bags and rubber bands for dirty clothes, shoes, keeping
ants out of foodstuff etc.
Camera and film
Electric jug with multi-plug and plastic mug
Multi-purpose knife and spoon
Portable washing line and detergent powder
Plug for bath or wash basin
Reading material
Spare visa photos
Business cards

Tickets
Passport and visas
Travellers cheques and local money

- Your travel checklist will vary depending on which countries you are visiting and the standard of your accommodation.
- Travel as light as you can. In most countries you can buy what you forget. Your cabin bag should contain a change of underclothes and essential toilet items in case your main luggage goes astray.
- Work out how much money you will need. Decide on a realistic daily allowance. Find out which credit cards are acceptable in the countries you will visit.
- Purchase travellers cheques and list their numbers in two different places.
- Try to purchase some of your destination's currency before you leave home – at least enough money to get you to your accommodation.
- Take half as many clothes and twice as much money as you think you will need!
- Use a very strong suitcase – preferably one with wheels. Fabric suitcases rip easily. Use special markings or colourful straps on your suitcase so you can identify it quickly.
- Start out with plenty of room in your suitcase for purchases.
- Make sure your shoes have been 'broken in' and are comfortable.
- If you wear spectacles or contact lenses, take spares.
- If you are going on a long flight, start adjusting your sleeping schedule a few days before you leave home to help reduce jet lag.
- Don't carry your valuables in a handbag. Wear your money and passport in a light-weight cotton money belt. Keep cash separate from credit cards, travellers cheques and passport.
- Keep your passport number and the date of issue handy – you'll need it often for completing entry forms.
- When you arrive, check your valuables into the hotel safe.

On long international flights
- Book in early at the airport so you have a choice of seat. If you

want to read or sleep get a window seat far away from the engines. If you plan to work with papers you will have more room in an aisle seat.

- Carry ear plugs, eye shades, necessary toilet gear, slippers (or thick socks) and medication in your hand luggage.
- Eat and drink alcohol modestly on the plane. Drink plenty of water, fruit juices and non-alcoholic beverages.
- Go to the toilet before meals are served. There are often long queues after the meal.
- Walk around the aisles periodically to help your blood circulation.
- Find out the customs restrictions before you arrive in a country. Know what imports are prohibited and how much alcohol and how many cigarettes you can take in free of duty.
- Never lose your temper with customs or immigration officials, however great the provocation. Polite, friendly cooperation will get you through more quickly.

In foreign countries

- Ask your travel agent about local customs in the countries you will visit and respect these customs. Be sensitive to local dress codes. Shorts are often unacceptable. Women should dress appropriately in Islamic countries. The length of men's hair can cause problems, too. In some countries you do not pass food or money with your left hand.
- Change your money at banks. There is usually a bank at the airport. You will get better rates than in hotels or shops. Keep the documentation.
- Get local advice on approximate taxi fares and negotiate fares before you start. In some countries where the taxi-drivers do not speak English it helps to have your destination written out in the local language. Ask for a receipt for your fare – this often brings the price down.
- In many countries it is not advisable to drink tap water unless you have boiled it. Bottled water marketed by reputable firms is safer for drinking and cleaning your teeth. Take water purifying tablets.
- Don't have ice in your drinks, even in the larger hotels. It may

have been made with contaminated water.
- Be wary of salads and raw foods in restaurants in tropical countries. It is safer to eat cooked vegetables and fruits you can peel yourself.
- It is handy to have your own tea- and coffee-making equipment. A small electric jug with a 'multi-plug' (one that can be adjusted to fit different power outlets) can be a good investment.
- Pay your hotel bill early. This gives you time to check it before you leave.
- Save enough local currency to pay your departure tax.

Warnings
- Don't forget to reconfirm your flight bookings.
- Don't wear clothing that sets you apart from the locals.
- Don't tell people you are new in the town.
- Carry shoulder bags diagonally across your shoulder, and on the side away from the kerb.
- Leave your travel agent's travel bag at home. On the streets it marks you as a tourist and a target for thieves.
- Don't carry a lot of jewellery. It is safer in your bank at home.
- Don't volunteer to shop for others. It can be time-consuming and stressful.
- *Never* carry parcels home as a favour for chance acquaintances. You may regret it when you reach Customs.

Visual aids

Improve your presentation. Slides and transparencies should be:

- Simple.
- Easy to understand.
- Able to be seen by the whole audience.

Other points to note:

- Each visual aid should have a single message.

- Use title phrases on charts and diagrams. For example 'Gross Income' *not* 'Graph 1'.
- Rehearse your talk with your visual aids before the event.
- Allow time for the audience to study each visual.
- Switch the projector off when you want to get the audience's attention.
- Don't use too many visual aids – just a few good ones.
- For details give a handout *after* you have finished talking.

See also *Lectures*, page 63.

A good visual aid can save you a lot of talking.

Write for easy reading

Keep it simple and lively. Most people are lazy readers, so if you want to write to be read, follow these simple rules.

Before you start, think about your readers
What would they be interested in? Write to arouse their interest or stir their imagination.

Plan and outline
Prepare a plan and outline what you want to say. Put your main points in logical order so your ideas flow from one point to the next.

Your opening paragraph
Catch the reader's attention with a bold statement or a story. Make them want to read on.

First a rough draft
Amplify your outline – put 'flesh on the bones'. Pretend you are talking to your readers as you write. The important thing is to get your ideas down.

Polish your script
Be prepared to write and rewrite several times until it flows smoothly.

Write crisply
- Use simple words and short sentences.
- Make your writing lively. Use strong, positive words and active verbs.
- Be enthusiastic. Share your emotions.
- Write to express, not to impress. Write as you would speak. Develop your own style. (Meaning is more important than style.)
- Write about people. Tell stories, relate anecdotes and share experiences.
- Use dialogue. Quotation marks attract attention, so use dialogue to emphasise special points. Invent people – invent conversations to add variety to your writing.

Paragraphs
Vary the length of your paragraphs, but generally keep them short.

Lively pages
Leave plenty of white spaces to break up your text. There is nothing more daunting than a book or a report with long chapters made up of long paragraphs.

Edit ... edit ... edit
Remove all unnecessary words and phrases, jargon and clichés. Make sure your meanings are clear and there are no ambiguous statements. Be ruthless – chop and change and rearrange statements until your writing sounds right to your ear. Check and re-check spelling, grammar and punctuation.

Your final draft
When you are satisfied, give your draft to a colleague for comments and helpful criticism. With their fresh approach, they may find errors and omissions.